GO EXTREME!

BE A PRO SKATEBOARDER

By Lynda Arnez

Gareth Stevens Publishing

Please visit our website, www.garethstevens.com. For a free color catalog of all our high-quality books, call toll free 1-800-542-2595 or fax 1-877-542-2596.

Library of Congress Cataloging-in-Publication Data
Names: Arnéz, Lynda, author.
Title: Be a pro skateboarder / Lynda Arnez.
Description: Buffalo, N.Y. : Gareth Stevens Publishing, [2024] | Series: Go extreme! | Includes bibliographical references and index.
Identifiers: LCCN 2023006833 | ISBN 9781538286968 (library binding) | ISBN 9781538286951 (paperback) | ISBN 9781538286975 (ebook)
Subjects: LCSH: Skateboarding–Juvenile literature. | Skateboarders–Juvenile literature.
Classification: LCC GV859.8 .A75 2024 | DDC 796.22–dc23/eng/20230216
LC record available at https://lccn.loc.gov/2023006833

First Edition

Published in 2024 by
Gareth Stevens Publishing
2544 Clinton St
Buffalo, NY 14224

Designer: Ellen Weber
Editor: Kristen Rajczak Nelson

Photo credits: Cover, p. 1 lzf/Shutterstock.com; p. 5 Arturo Verea/Shutterstock.com; p. 7, 23 A.RICARDO/Shutterstock.com; p. 9, 27 Dean Drobot/Shutterstock.com; p. 11 hurricanehank/Shutterstock.com; p. 13 Kathy Hutchins/Shutterstock.com; p. 15 Stig Nygaard/Wikimedia Commons, https://commons.wikimedia.org/w/index.php?curid=47210484; p. 17 Rick Becker-Leckrone/Shutterstock.com; p. 19 Cristalitos Studios/Shutterstock.com; p. 21 FiledIMAGE/Shutterstock.com; p. 25 Kseniya Bogdanova/Shutterstock.com; p. 27 Dean Drobot/Shutterstock.com; p. 29 kornnphoto/Shutterstock.com; Series Art Mind Pixell/Shutterstock.com; Series Art Duda Vasilii/Shutterstock.com; Series Art PegasuStudio/Shutterstock.com; Series Art Scott Webb/Pexels.

Printed in the United States of America

CPSIA compliance information: Batch #CS24GS: For further information contact Gareth Stevens, New York, New York at 1-800-542-2595.

CONTENTS

A BIG DREAM

Skateboarding superstar Tony Hawk was 9 when his brother gave him his first skateboard. He turned pro at age 14 and began to win any **contest** he was in. It's an incredible story! But, for most skateboarders, the road to going pro is a bit longer.

PUSHING THE LIMITS

Street style includes skating and doing tricks in an area like a city street. Vert includes using U-shaped **ramps** called half-pipes and doing tricks in the air.

Tony Hawk

WHAT DOES "PRO" MEAN?

Pro is short for "professional." It means getting paid to do something for a job. In skateboarding, though, it also may have to do with winning contests and taking part in certain **competitions**. Some contests only allow pros to compete too.

PUSHING THE LIMITS

Skateboarding became part of the Olympics in the games held in 2021 in Tokyo, Japan.

GET STARTED!

Every pro started by stepping on a skateboard. If you've never tried skateboarding before, you might be able to find classes to take where you live. At first, your goal should be to simply get better every time you skate!

PUSHING THE LIMITS

Skateboarding gear includes a skateboard, a special helmet, wrist guards, elbow and knee pads, and shoes with a closed toe that don't slip.

Just like any sport, some people have a natural **talent** for skateboarding. Still, everyone must work hard if they want to be a pro someday! Learning new skills—like your first trick—takes time, **patience**, and practice.

PUSHING THE LIMITS

Skateboarders fall a lot. They get injured, or hurt. Learning the basics, wearing the right safety gear, and following the rules in the skatepark will help keep you safe.

START COMPETING

You'll need to learn tricks before you start competing. Once you feel ready, enter a contest. Every contest is good **experience**, no matter how you do. It's also a great way to connect with people in your local skate community.

PUSHING THE LIMITS

Champion skateboarder Nyjah Huston first entered the X Games at 11 years old!

Nyjah Huston

HOW DO YOU GET PAID?

You need to stand out to get noticed by sponsors. Skateboarding team managers are always on the lookout for new talent. They work for **brands** that make skateboarding gear and apparel, or clothing. Winning contests is one way to stand out!

PUSHING THE LIMITS

A sponsor is a brand or company that gives a person gear, clothing, or money in exchange for different kinds of **promotion**.

In the past, making a video a few minutes long and sending it to team managers was a way to get sponsors. This is still the case sometimes. But now, social media is an even more common way for skateboarders to show off their skills.

PUSHING THE LIMITS

You can try and connect with brands you want to work for online or in person at skateboarding contests.

A skateboarder's social media following is important to sponsors. The more followers they have, the more people will see the brands they promote. Their image is shaped by what they post. Brands will be drawn in by positive, **authentic** skaters with their own style!

PUSHING THE LIMITS

Your image is how people see you. Sponsors are looking for people with an image that makes sense with theirs.

LEVELS OF SPONSORSHIP

Skateboarding can be an expensive, or costly, sport. One way brands sponsor skateboarders is through a "flow" sponsorship. This means a brand might send boards, shoes, or parts for skateboards. This is often the first kind of sponsorship a pro gets.

PUSHING THE LIMITS

Getting a board sponsor—or a company that gives you boards for your skateboard—is the marker for many that a skater has turned pro!

Amateur usually means not professional. In skateboarding, though, amateur sponsorship means you are part of a skate team. These sponsors help their skaters enter big contests around the world! Doing well at certain amateur contests qualifies skaters for the biggest pro contests.

PUSHING THE LIMITS

There are both big brands and small brands that offer sponsorships. Skaters have to decide what kind of company is a good fit to work with.

True pro skateboarders are commonly the best skaters in the world. They earn prize money for winning in addition to having sponsorship. Skate teams may pay them as well as covering their contest fees and travel and giving them free gear.

PUSHING THE LIMITS

Pro skateboarders can make a living skating. But few make the millions of dollars other sports stars earn. Many have other jobs they do besides skating.

GET ADVICE!

Who better to get tips from than a pro? Many pro skateboarders offer lessons. See if you can find a pro or a coach to help you get to the next level. They might be the one to discover your talent!

PUSHING THE LIMITS

Skateboarding is hard on the body. Staying fit, including running, swimming, and lifting weights, helps skateboarders keep from getting hurt.

LOVE IT!

Many pros say it takes a lot of luck to become one of the biggest skateboarders in the world. So, young skateboarders should just try to have fun! Spend as much time skating as you can. Learn new tricks and do what you love!

PUSHING THE LIMITS

Some skateboarders make money without doing contests. These "social" skaters have big social media followings and promote brands on their pages.

LEARN THE LINGO

aerial
a trick done with all four wheels off the ground or ramp

backside
a trick or turn that is done backwards, or with the skater facing away from the ramp or surface

bail
to end a trick by stepping or jumping off the board, or kicking the board away midair hoping to land safely

drop in
to go from the flat top of a ramp into the ramp. It can also mean something skaters can drop in to.

frontside
describing when a trick or turn is done facing the ramp or surface to be skated on

land
to finish a trick successfully

session
a time skaters gather to skate

slam
falling hard

FOR MORE INFORMATION

BOOKS

Boswell, Bettie. *Skateboarding.* Mendota Heights, MN: Apex, 2022.

Lyon, Drew. *Big-Time Extreme Sports Records.* North Mankato, MN: Capstone Press, 2022.

WEBSITES

The Official Site of USA Skateboarding
usaskateboarding.com/
Follow USA Skateboarding to find out more about competitions and the Olympics.

Safety Tips: Skateboarding
kidshealth.org/en/parents/safety-skateboarding.html
Check out these tips to stay safe as you hop on your board!

GLOSSARY

authentic: Real and true.

brand: A group of products made by a company under a certain name.

competition: A contest in which you try to win against others.

contest: An event at which people try to win by being better than others.

experience: The act of doing or seeing things or having things happen to you.

patience: The ability to wait.

promotion: The act of furthering or advancing something, often the sale of certain items through advertising. Promote means to make people aware of.

ramp: A piece of equipment that has a slope joining two surfaces that are different heights.

talent: Having the skills to do something well. Also, those who have the skills to do something well.

INDEX